Also by BRUCE JAY FRIEDMAN

The Dick

Scuba Duba (a play)

Black Angels (stories)

A Mother's Kisses

Far From the City of Class (stories)

Stern

STEAMBATH

STEAMBATH

BRUCE JAY FRIEDMAN

A PLAY

Alfred A. Knopf   New York   1971

Photographs by courtesy of Ted Yaple

ISBN: 0–394–46904–6
Library of Congress Catalog Number: 74–136323
Manufactured in the United States of America

FIRST EDITION

To my friends at the
North Shore Athletic Club

STEAMBATH *was presented by Ivor David Balding for the 54th Street Landlord Company, Inc., at the Truck and Warehouse Theatre, New York City, on June 30, 1970. Directed by Anthony Perkins. Scenery by David Mitchell. Costumes by Joseph G. Aulisi. Lighting by Jules Fisher. Special Visual Effects by Marvin Torffield. Choreography by Grover Dale. Associate Producer Richard Scanga.*

THE CAST

TANDY	Anthony Perkins
MORTY	Hector Elizondo
BIEBERMAN	Marvin Lichterman
MEREDITH	Annie Rachel
OLDTIMER	Conrad Bain
BROKER	Mitchell Jason
YOUNG MAN	Jere Admire
YOUNG MAN	Teno Pollick
GOTTLIEB	Gabor Morea
FIRST LONGSHOREMAN	Jack Knight
YOUNG GIRL	Eileen Dietz
FLANDERS	Alfred Hickley

Setting: A Steambath
Time: The Present

A steamroom. Benches or slabs and a single overhead shower. Effect of steam is achieved by either steam or light or both. People speak, disappear in the haze, reappear. Characters are costumed in sheets or cloths or something in between. At the beginning of the action, a young man (thirty-five to forty-five) enters and sits down next to an OLDTIMER. *He is ever so slightly puzzled by his surroundings but does his best to conceal this mild concern. He has a great deal of trouble when he makes contact with the hot seat.*

OLDTIMER: That's really something, isn't it, when you sit down?

TANDY: It's a bitch.

OLDTIMER: It don't bother me. When you're a young fellow, it bothers you, but then you develop a tough ass.

TANDY: I knew your beard got tough, but I didn't realize the other thing . . .

OLDTIMER: It's true.

>   (THEY *sit awhile*)

I've had some wonderful sweats in my time.

TANDY: That right?

OLDTIMER: Oh yeah. When the Polish came in, the union gave them a steambath down on Fulton Street . . . Nobody sweats like the Polish . . . What you're doing now . . .

TANDY (*Feeling himself*): Yes?

OLDTIMER: That's garbage. You're not sweatin' . . . I never exercised much, though. You see this area here. (*Pulls flesh in his lower back region*) I always wanted to keep that nice and soft in case I got some spinal trouble. So the needle could go right in. I know guys, athletes, they're so hard you can't stick a needle into them . . . I figure it's a good idea to keep it soft back there.

>   (THEY *sit awhile longer*)

How do you feel about heart attacks?

TANDY: I'm against them.

OLDTIMER: Lot of people are. I'll say this for them, though. They don't mark you on the outside. They leave you clean as a whistle. That's more than you can say for a gall bladder.

TANDY: I agree with you there.

OLDTIMER: I seen guys get cut up for ulcers they got bellies look like the map of downtown Newark, New Jersey . . . People have always been a little too rough on heart attacks. The heart attack's always gotten a raw deal.

> (BIEBERMAN, *an unattractive fellow, concealed behind a pillar, clears his throat and then spits on the floor*)

Hey, I saw that.

BIEBERMAN: What?

OLDTIMER: You know what. What you did. Expectorating like that. It's disgusting.

BIEBERMAN: What's wrong? It's a natural fluid.

OLDTIMER: You're a disgrace. (*To* TANDY) You got to watch him like a hawk. Probably farting back there, too. Who the hell would ever know in a steambath.

BIEBERMAN (*Still concealed*): I heard that. I'm not farting.

OLDTIMER: Congratulations . . .

BIEBERMAN: My generation doesn't do that.

OLDTIMER: Your generation can kiss my ass. (*To* TANDY) What's your line, young fella?

TANDY: I just quit my job. I was teaching art appreciation over at the Police Academy.

OLDTIMER: That right. What the hell . . . I guess you got to do something. Police, eh? Ever notice how you never get any trouble from the good people?

TANDY: Well, that's for sure.

OLDTIMER: It's the bad ones you got to watch. You run the bad ones off the street that'll be the end of your crime. You got a son?

TANDY: No, I've got a little girl.

OLDTIMER: You got a son, I hope he's a drunk. That'll keep him off drugs. He starts in on that dope stuff you can kiss his ass goodbye. (*In reference to* BIEBERMAN) What's that guy doing now?

TANDY (*Checking behind pillar*): Looks like he's eating an orange.

OLDTIMER: Yeah, but what's he *doing?*

TANDY (*Checks again, gets hit by a fusillade of pits*): He's spitting out the pits.

OLDTIMER: Stupid mother. (*Shouting to* BIEBERMAN) Hey, knock it off, will you?

BIEBERMAN: Well, what am I supposed to do with them?

OLDTIMER: Hold them in your hand. Swallow them. Shove them up your ass, what do I care. Just don't spit them out. Didn't you ever hear of a person tripping on pits? (*To* TANDY) They get some crowd in here. He's probably a fag, too.

TWO YOUNG MEN (*Invisible, speaking in unison*): No, we're the fags.

OLDTIMER: I beg your pardon. (*More or less to himself*) I knew there were fags in here. (*To* TANDY) You broke a sweat yet, son?

TANDY: I can feel one coming.

OLDTIMER: You know what would go down really well now? A nice cool brew.

> (A BAR BOY *enters with two cold beers and glasses. In later appearances, he is referred to as* GOTTLIEB. TANDY *and the* OLDTIMER *each take a beer and begin to sip at it.*)

I drank a lot of beer in my time. One thing I'll say for myself is that I never gained weight. I gained bloat. The trouble is—bloat weighs a lot too. Most people don't realize that. Bloat can kill you.

TANDY: What do you do?

OLDTIMER: I done a lot of things. In my late years I took to hackin' a cab. I was terrific once I got my daily ice-breaker. But until then I wasn't fit to live with. That's how I had my crash—worried sick about getting my icebreaker. I come on the job at eight in the morning, it's twelve o'clock noon I still hadn't nailed a fare. I'm so upset I drive right through a furrier's window. Into the beaver pelts, I wound up with the car radio in my stomach. And I mean in my stomach, too. I had folk music coming out of my asshole. So that was it.

TANDY: That was it?

OLDTIMER: That was it.

> (*A beautiful young girl comes forth, wearing a sheet, humming a tune.* SHE *is very blonde. Matter-of-factly* SHE *drops the sheet, steps beneath the shower and pulls the shower chain. Little cry of alarm when the water hits her, but* SHE *enjoys it.* SHE *puts the sheet back on and disappears in the*) *haze.*)

TANDY: She come in here often?

OLDTIMER: Can't say. Nice set of maracas on her, though.

TANDY: Damn right.

OLDTIMER: You know, a lot of guys let the little old frank-furter rule their heads. I always say, let your head rule the little old frankfurter. You go along with that?

TANDY (*After thinking it over*): Yeah! Well . . .

OLDTIMER: I never forget this rich bitch on Long Island had her eye on me. I said, madame, that little old weenie you're so interested in don't run the show. I'm the one that runs the show. She didn't like that.

TANDY (*Distracted*): That was unusual.

OLDTIMER: What's that?

TANDY: That girl. Taking a shower that way.

OLDTIMER: Nah, they got everything today. I got a son-in-law got two toilets in one bathroom. He puts my two young granddaughters on there, puts a tape recorder between them and records what they say to each other while on the pot. That's my son-in-law's idea of a laugh.

TANDY: Is that right . . .

OLDTIMER: I knew I was going to have trouble with him.

(*The* TWO YOUNG MEN *come down and do a dancing and singing musical number from a popular Broadway musical comedy, complete with intricate steps, high kicks—in perfect unison.* THEY *have a little Panasonic-type player, of the cheap 42nd Street variety. This is the source of the music.* THEY *are quite good, semi-professional.* THEY *finish up big and then go back to their seats*)

TANDY: This is some place.

OLDTIMER: Lucky they didn't slip on the pits.

(*Hoarse, guttural sound in the back, suspiciously from* BIEBERMAN'*s direction*)

OLDTIMER: What are you doing now?

BIEBERMAN: Gargling. I have a rough throat.

OLDTIMER: That's what I was afraid of. You watch your step, meathead. (*To* TANDY) He starts blowing his nose, I'm going after him . . .

TANDY: They were very good. The dancers.

OLDTIMER: They do some good work. I never could enjoy a show much. I was always more interested in what was going on in the wings. I figured the real show, the good stuff, was going on back there. I'd rather sit and watch the wings than your top show on Broadway.

TANDY: I'd rather watch a show. I've never been that interested in the wings. But I see what you mean.

(BLONDE GIRL *approaches*)

MEREDITH: Are you all right?

TANDY: I'm fine. How was your shower?

MEREDITH: It was wonderful. Some day I'd like to meet the man who invented the needle-point showerhead and thank him for all the pleasure he's given me.

TANDY: Do you come here often?

MEREDITH: I don't know. All I can remember is that I was buying this little skirt at Paraphernalia . . . it couldn't have been this big and they were asking $17.50 for it—

BIEBERMAN (*Appearing for the first time, on a ledge above* TANDY *and* MEREDITH. HE *speaks with a certain stopped-up anger*): You have no idea what those skirts have meant to members of my generation. What a skirt like that means to a fellow who could sit through the same movie seven times, willing to sell himself into bondage on a farm in Mississippi if he could see just an eighth of an inch of Ann Rutherford's inner thigh. And then there they are, out of the blue, those pitzel cocker skirts. And the girls wearing them, more beautiful than Ann Rutherford herself, are handing out massive looks at their thighs and crotches. No one has properly realized the effect of all that exposed and quivering flesh on the national character. And my generation is condemned to watch this country, representing one of the greatest social experiments in Western civilization, choke itself to death on an easy diet of tits and asses.

TANDY: Look, do you mind? We were having a private conversation . . .

BIEBERMAN: As you wish.

> (HE *drops his sheet, and, in his jockey shorts, begins to do a vigorous exercise, disgustingly close to* TANDY *and* MEREDITH)

TANDY: Do you have to do that here?

OLDTIMER: He's just getting warmed up.

BIEBERMAN: It's just till I work up a good healthy sweat.

TANDY: Do it somewhere else, will you.

BIEBERMAN (*Under his breath, as he moves off*): Putz.

TANDY (*Starting to chase* BIEBERMAN): Hey! (*To* OLD-TIMER) He *is* disgusting. I never saw it until just now.

MEREDITH: You were a little hard on him.

TANDY: Was I? I didn't realize it. I was with the cops for a while. In the cultural section. I still have a little of the cop style left.

MEREDITH: Listen, if you were with the cops, could you tell me exactly where to kick someone so that he's temporarily paralyzed and can't rape you—yet at the same time doesn't feel you're an insensitive person . . .

TANDY: We stayed away from that stuff in the art department . . . What really puzzles me is that I am able to talk to you so easily.

MEREDITH: What do you mean?

TANDY: Well, until recently, I had a great deal of trouble talking to yellow-haired girls. I felt I had to talk to them in verse or something . . . maybe wear special gloves. But apparently I've gotten over that.

MEREDITH: You're so nice. I love meeting a nice new person like you. But look, I don't want to get involved.

TANDY: Involved?

MEREDITH: I just can't go through with that again . . . I've had that this year . . . the phone calls . . . My skin . . . For what it does to my skin alone, it's not worth it . . . Look, I just don't have the strength for another affair . . . Maybe around Labor Day . . . If it's worth anything, it'll be good then, too . . . Will you call me then?

TANDY (*Thinks awhile*): I'll give you a ring.

MEREDITH: You're not angry, are you?

TANDY: I'm not angry.

MEREDITH: It's got nothing to do with you personally . . . you seem like a very sensual person.

OLDTIMER: There is a terrible stink in here. And I got a pretty good idea who's responsible for it.

BIEBERMAN: I haven't done a thing recently.

OLDTIMER: You'll never convince me of that. Whatever you're doing, cut it out—for my sake, for the sake of this steambath, and for the sake of America.

BIEBERMAN: I'm just sitting here, being natural, being myself . . .

OLDTIMER: That's what it is? Natural? . . . That's what you've got to stop.

TANDY (*To* MEREDITH): Listen, what do you think of this place?

MEREDITH: I like it.

TANDY: Notice anything peculiar about it?

MEREDITH: It smells a little funny.

OLDTIMER: It sure as hell does.

BIEBERMAN: I haven't done a thing. I've been doing a cross-
word puzzle. (*To* TANDY) What's a six-letter word that
means little red spikes of corn?

OLDTIMER: How about "giggie"? Used in a sentence, it
goes: "Up your giggie."

BIEBERMAN: Lovely.

> (*Lights darken. A screen drops. Stock quo-
> tations flash across the screen as they do in
> a brokerage office. A fellow appears with a
> chair, sits down opposite the screen, and
> watches the quotations*)

BROKER (*Taking notes*): They put that in for me.

TANDY: How's the market?

BROKER: Lousy. If you own good stocks. When I went into
this business, I had one piece of advice for every one of
my customers: "Put your money in good stuff. Stay

away from shit. That's what you want, find yourself another broker. I don't touch it." So what happens in the last five years? The good stuff lays there, shit goes right through the roof. Some of my customers, they went to other brokers, they bought shit, they made fortunes . . .

MEREDITH (*Very trusting*): Maybe the good stuff will improve. If it's really and truly good.

BROKER: Nah . . . It's too late for that . . .

(*Screen disappears.* HE *picks up chair, recedes into the haze*)

TANDY: That's the kind of thing I was talking about . . .

MEREDITH: What do you mean?

TANDY: A guy like that . . . in here . . . watching stocks . . . it's strange.

MEREDITH: I just wish the numbers wouldn't go by so fast. You hardly have any time to enjoy them. Am I wrong or have you been doing pretty well lately?

TANDY: I'm doing fine. I got a divorce. I quit the Police Academy. I'm writing a novel about Charlemagne. And I just got involved in a charity. Helping brain-damaged welders. I was looking for a charity and that's the one I picked. They send out a terrific brochure. There are an awful lot of them . . . welders . . . with brain damage . . . and they're really grateful when you help them. You should see the looks on some of those welders' faces. Could break your heart . . . I've been doing pretty well . . . I'm real close to my ten-year-old daughter.

MEREDITH: You have a ten-year-old daughter?

TANDY: Oh yeah, we just got back from Vegas.

MEREDITH: How did she like it?

TANDY: Well, she thought little girls were allowed to gamble out there. She insisted that somewhere in Vegas there were slot machines that little girls were allowed to play. Well, I read that you shouldn't disabuse a child of its fantasies, so I went along with the gag. So we spent four days looking for these special slot machines. Finally, when we got to the airport, I told her that little girls were allowed to play the airport slots just before they got on the plane. She said, "I told you, Daddy." We got very close on that trip. So I've been doing pretty well lately . . .

MEREDITH: Listen, you don't think . . .

TANDY: What? What?

MEREDITH: All I can remember is that Sheila and I were buying skirts at Paraphernalia. Then we went back to our high-rise apartment on 84th Street and, oh, yes, the Gristede's delivery boy was waiting behind the drapes, with a crazy look on his face, holding a blunt instrument . . .

TANDY: I was in my favorite restaurant, eating some Chinese food. I was just about to knock off a double order of Won Shih pancakes . . .

MEREDITH: You don't think?

TANDY: . . . We're dead? Is that what you were going to say? That's what I was going to say. That's what we are. The second I said it, I knew it. Bam! Dead! Just like that! Christ!

MEREDITH: I had it pictured an entirely different way.

TANDY: What's that?

MEREDITH: Being dead. I thought dying meant that you'd have to spend every day of your life at a different Holiday Inn. Then I decided it was seeing *So Proudly We Hail* with Veronica Lake over and over for the rest of time. In a place where there were no Mounds bars.

> (VOICE *is heard:* "*Cold drinks, popcorn, Raisinettes, Goobers. And no Mounds bars*")

TANDY: Don't pay any attention. Somebody's kidding around.

MEREDITH (*With real loss*): No Mounds bars . . .

TANDY: I don't know about you, but I'm not accepting this.

MEREDITH: What do you mean?

TANDY: I don't like the whole way it was done. Bam. Dead. Just like that. Just like you're a schmuck or something.

MEREDITH: What are you going to do?

TANDY: I'll do something. Don't worry. I'm a doer. If you had any idea of the agony I went through to change my life around you'd see why I'm so pissed off. To be picked off like this when I haven't even started to enjoy the good stuff.

MEREDITH: Well, how about me? I just had my first orgasm.

TANDY: Just now?

MEREDITH: No. While I was watching the David Frost Show. I was all alone, eating some Whip and Chill and I got this funny feeling.

TANDY: I'll tell you right now, I'm not going along with it. Not now. Not when I'm just getting off the ground. Another time, later on, they want me to be dead, fine. Not now. Uh-uh.

MEREDITH: I feel exactly the same way. How can I die? I haven't even bought any vinyl bust harnesses. And I've got to get my thighs down. Everything I eat has a little sign on it that says, "Do not pass go. Move directly to thighs." No, I absolutely can't die. Is there something you can do?

TANDY: I'll check around, see if I can find out something.

(*Disappears in haze*)

OLDTIMER (*Reading newspaper*): Says here they got a new gas, one gallon of it'll wipe out an entire enemy country . . .

BROKER: They got more than that. They got another one— just one drop in the water supply and the whole continent starts vomiting.

OLDTIMER (*Sniffing*): They could bottle the smell around here, they don't need any gas. You hear that back there?

BIEBERMAN: I'm not doing anything. I'm working on my toes.

OLDTIMER: I knew it, the son of a bitch. What are you doing to them?

BIEBERMAN: Trimming down the nails.

OLDTIMER: In here? This is where you picked? Cut it out will you, you slob, you're trying my patience.

TANDY (*Taking aside* OLDTIMER): Can I see you a second, Oldtimer?

OLDTIMER: What's on your mind, fella? Havin' trouble breathin'? (*Demonstrating*) Suck it in through your mouth awhile.

TANDY: I was sitting over there with this girl . . .

OLDTIMER (*Lasciviously*): The one with them Chitty-Chitty Bang-Bangs?

TANDY: That's the one.

OLDTIMER: Don't let her get hold of your liverwurst. They get an armlock on that they never let go.

TANDY: I got the idea that we were dead. And she agrees with me. Now I can take the dead part. That doesn't scare me. I get older, a little tired, fine. I even thought maybe later on, things go smoothly, maybe I'll knock myself off. Make it simple. But the timing's all wrong now. I'm just getting off the ground. I'm in the middle of writing an historical novel. Right in the fucking middle. (I don't talk this way in the book.) It's about Charlemagne. I've got a great new girl friend cooks me shish kebab. Bryn Mawr girl. And she still cooks shish kebab. Doesn't bother her a bit. And I never think about Wendy.

OLDTIMER: Wendy?

TANDY: My ex-wife. Wendy Tandy. Jesus, I just realized, she was Wendy Hilton, I turned her into Wendy Tandy. I probably blew the whole marriage right there. She never went for that name. Can't say that I blame her. Anyway, I don't think about her anymore. Weeks at a time. She could be out fucking the whole Royal Canadian Mounties I don't give it a thought. I forgive her. She's a little weak. It's got nothing to do with me. So, you see, I'm really just starting a wonderful new chapter of my life. And along comes this death number —I thought maybe you could help me . . .

OLDTIMER: I hardly know what to say to you, fella. You come at me like a ten-foot wave.

TANDY: Is there a guy in charge? Somebody I can talk to. E. G. Marshall? Walter Pidgeon?

OLDTIMER: There's a guy comes around. I see him I'll point him out.

TANDY: Thanks. You're not a bad skate. When we get out of this, maybe we can pal around together.

OLDTIMER: You probably smell the sea on me. Before I took up hackin' I worked the China coast for seventeen years. Me and my friend Ollie were the most widely respected duo west of Macao. We'd get ourselves a couple of juki-juki girls, take 'em up on deck and do a little missionary work with 'em anchored in front of Bruce Wong's Monkey Meat Shop in Hong Kong Harbor. They arrested Ollie for abusing himself into the holy water fountain at the Merchant Seaman's Chapel. He died in irons and I lost the best friend I ever had . . .

(*Fades off, a bit overcome with emotion*)

MEREDITH: What did that old man say?

TANDY: He said there's a fellow around who seems to be in charge. That he'd point him out to me. Listen, how do you feel?

MEREDITH: I don't mind being nude, if that's what you mean. I just don't attribute that much importance to it.

TANDY: I know that. I can tell.

MEREDITH: I wouldn't want to get out there and do splits or anything.

TANDY: Who asked you to do splits? Is that what you think I want—splits?

MEREDITH: I just like to be nude sometimes. It's very tranquil.

TANDY: You see, that's where I really got a bum steer. The fellow who first taught me about sex—very smart guy, been all over, a Socialist—he told me, "Remember one thing, kid, women feel uncomfortable about being nude." So for a long time I went around covering up nude girls. They'd say, "What the hell are you doing?" and I'd say, "C'mon, I know you're uncomfortable." And I was wrong. I covered up some gorgeous women.

(*A Puerto Rican* ATTENDANT *has been mopping up the steambath for awhile.* HE *comes clearly into view now.* HE *sings "Sorrento." Lah lah lah lah sentimento . . . lah lah lah lah sentirinco . . . lah lah lah lah ladimento . . . lah lah lah lah lah lah lah. Stops mopping to do the bridge, really performing now . . . lah lah lah lah lah lah . . . etc. After a big finish,* HE *says, "Thank you, music lovers" as though to a nightclub audience . . .*)

OLDTIMER (*Signaling to* TANDY): Psssst.

TANDY (*Gesturing toward* ATTENDANT): Him?

(OLDTIMER *acknowledges correctness with a wink*)

You sure?

OLDTIMER: Yup . . .

TANDY (*To* MEREDITH): He says that's the fellow in charge.

MEREDITH: He's cute.

ATTENDANT: Hiya, baby.

> (ATTENDANT *now wheels out what appears to be a console with a screen. It is a very tacky-looking affair. The screen is visible to the* ATTENDANT *but not to the audience. The console, from time to time, answers the* ATTENDANT *with little blipping noises as though taking note of his instructions. In between sections of his monologue, the Puerto Rican does little snatches of "Sorrento" again*)

(*Leaning over console*) San Diego Freeway . . . All right, first thing, I want that Pontiac moving south past Hermosa Beach to crash into the light blue Eldorado coming the other way. Make it a head-on collision . . . the guy in the Chevy—his wife's got her ass out the window—it's the only way they get their kicks—they're going to jump the rail into the oncoming lane, and fuck up a liquor salesman in a tan Cougar. No survivors . . .

All right, what's-his-name, Perez, the Puerto Rican schmuck from the Bronx. The one who says, "My wife and I—we are married forty years. We are born on the same hill. There can be no trouble." He comes home tonight, I want her screwing her brother. Perez walks in, goes crazy, starts foaming at the mouth, the other tenants in the building have to tie him to a radiator . . .

All right, the guy from St. Louis . . . bedspread salesman . . . adopted all those Korean kids. Him they pick up in the men's room of the Greyhound Bus Terminal, grabbing some truckdriver's schvontz. They ask around, find out he's been doing it for years . . . The kids get shipped back to Korea.

Now, here's one I like . . . The screenwriter flying out to Beverly Hills. Coming on with the broads. Here's what happens. Over Denver, a stewardess throws a dart in his eye. No doctor on board. He has to go all the way to Los Angeles like that. Pheww! . . .

The hooker—little fat one—been peddling her ass in Barcelona for three years—took on 4,000 sailors—she's saved up a few bucks, she's gonna go straight. Get ready. This is rough. I want her found in a dirt pit on Montauk Highway. And if her parents really carry on, I mean really piss and moan, then go after the sister, too, the homely one. Give her an ear infection.

Now, the producer up in New Haven. Never had a hit. Doing a $750,000 musical . . . the whole show depends on the female star. All right. A police dog gets loose in the theatre and bites her tits off. The understudy is scared shit, but she goes on anyway. Bombsville. Next day, the guy gets out of the business . . .

(*Starts to leave, returns*)

Wait a minute. I got an idea. Back to the Freeway. That guy whose radiator boiled over . . . on the side of the road, saw the whole thing. Thought he got away clean. He gets knocked unconscious by the bare-assed broad. Never knew what hit him. That's all for now.

> (HE *picks up mop and continues to mop the steambath floor.* HE *sings "Sorrento." And* HE *disappears for the moment in the haze*)

TANDY: You sure that's the fellow in charge?

OLDTIMER: That's him all right. He runs the show.

TANDY: What's his name?

OLDTIMER: Morty.

TANDY: A Puerto Rican guy? Morty?

OLDTIMER: It's Spanish. (*Pronouncing name with Spanish inflection*) Mawwrrr-teee.

TANDY (*To* MEREDITH): He's sure that's the fellow in charge.

MEREDITH: Well if he isn't, he certainly has a rich imagination.

TANDY: You say he hangs around here.

OLDTIMER: All the time. He comes and goes.

(ATTENDANT *returns, singing softly, sweeping, goes to console again. His voice is much softer now*)

ATTENDANT: Okay, the other side of the coin. The kid in a hospital in Trenton, beautiful kid, works for Carvel's. Got his foot shot off in a stick-up. The night nurse comes in, jerks him off under the covers. Lovely broad, little old, but she really knows what she's doing . . .

Give Canada a little more rain . . .

That Indian tribe outside of Caracas. Sick little guys, they ain't got a hundred bucks between 'em . . . Government doesn't give a shit. CBS moves in, shoots a jungle series there, throws a lot of money around . . .

The old lady with the parakeet, flies out the window, flies back in . . .

Wellesley girl, parents got a lot of dough—she's sitting on a ledge—35th floor of the Edison Hotel. A cop crawls out after her, tells her she's a pain in the ass. They go back in, watch a hockey game on TV . . . And clean up that garbage in the lobby . . . It's disgusting . . .

That spade they beat up at Chicago Police headquarters. Got a landing strip for a head. All right, kill the cop who roughed him up—and then send the spade over to Copenhagen for a vacation. At least three months. I don't know who picks up the tab. He's got a cousin in the music business. Records for Decca . . .

All right, that's enough good stuff.

VOICE: You need one more.

ATTENDANT: Christ, I'm exhausted. Uhh . . . Put bigger bath towels in all the rooms at the Tel Aviv Hilton Hotel.

VOICE: Terrific!

ATTENDANT: You kidding, buddy . . .

(*Exits*)

MEREDITH: I liked him much more the second time.

TANDY: He's got some style. Who's he think he is?

OLDTIMER: God.

TANDY: You believe that?

OLDTIMER: I'm not saying yes and I'm not saying no. I been around and I seen a lot of strange things in my time. I once stood in an Algerian pissoir urinal and watched the head of a good friend of mine come rolling up against my size 12 moccasins like a bowling ball. Cut right off at the neck. He'd gotten into a little scuffle with some Gurkhas. May have called one of them a fag. Didn't know there aren't any fag Gurkhas.

TWO YOUNG MEN: That's what you think.

TANDY: Well, what the hell are we supposed to do, just stay here?

BROKER: There's nothing that great out there. The market stinks. You don't make a quarter unless you're in pork bellies. That ain't investing.

TANDY: I'm not going along with this. For Christ's sakes, I'm in the middle of writing an historical novel. About Charlemagne. I got all that research to do. So far I've been going on instinct. What the hell do I know about Charlemagne. But the book feels good . . .

MEREDITH: And I've got an appointment at the beauty parlor. To get a Joan of Arc haircut. And my room-mate Sheila and I are going to make little plastic surrealistic doodads and sell them to boutiques.

TANDY: I'll get us out of this. Did you try the door?

MEREDITH: No, why?

TANDY: Don't try it. I'm pretty sure it doesn't open. If I find out for sure I'll get claustrophobia . . . Is there another way out? What's this door? (*Referring to second door at opposite side of the stage*)

OLDTIMER: You go through there.

TANDY: When's that?

OLDTIMER: Hard to say . . . We had a guy, a baker, he put him in there.

TANDY: What did he do?

OLDTIMER: Not much. Beat the Puerto Rican in arm-wrestling.

BROKER: Had a little trouble with his baking though. Everything used to burn up on him. Pastries, cupcakes . . . meat pies . . .

TANDY: Don't tell me about cupcakes now . . . no cupcakes. When he puts you in there, does he let you out?

> (OLDTIMER *chuckles, as if to say, "Are you kidding?"*)

And that's it, the two doors?

OLDTIMER: That's it. That's the whole cheesecake.

> (TANDY *very casually sidles up to entrance door, tries it. It doesn't open. Tries a little harder. Still won't*)

TANDY: About the way I figured. I'll get us out of here, don't worry. You with me?

MEREDITH: Are you serious? Of course. But you haven't said how.

TANDY: I'll get us out. You'll find I do most things well. Of course, I have never been able to get out to Kennedy

Airport. On my own. I can get near it, but never really
in it. The Van Wyck Expressway scene really throws me.

MEREDITH: You're sort of inconsistent, aren't you?

TANDY: You noticed that, eh. I admit it. I've got wonderful
qualities, but getting out to airports is not one of them.
Don't worry, though, I'll get us out of here. By sheer
strength of will and determination. I believe I can do
anything if I really put my mind to it. I've always felt
that even if I had a fatal illness, with an army of dis-
eased phagocytes coursing through my body in
triumph, if I really decided to, I could reverse the
course of those phagocytes and push them the hell
back where they belong . . .

MEREDITH: The world admires that kind of determination.

TANDY: You're damned right.

MEREDITH: What if we really are dead, though?

TANDY: I know. I've been trying not to think about it. No
more toast. No more clams. Clams oregano.

MEREDITH: No more playing with Mr. Skeffington.

TANDY: Mr. Skeffington? Wait a minute, don't tell me.
That's your cat.

MEREDITH: Yes.

TANDY: How can you compare that in seriousness to the things I'm talking about? I'm talking about big stuff. No more sneezing. No more being under the covers. No more airline stewardesses . . . *Newsweek* . . . Jesus, no more *Newsweek*. Wait a minute, I'll get this straightened out right now . . . (HE *approaches* AT-TENDANT, *who has come mopping into view*) Say, fella . . .

ATTENDANT: You addressing I?

TANDY: That's right. What's the deal around here? The Old-timer says you're God.

ATTENDANT: Some people call me that.

TANDY: But that's ridiculous . . . a Puerto Rican . . .

ATTENDANT: The Puerto Ricans go back hundreds of years. Millions. There were Puerto Ricans in Greece, Rome. Diogenes—very big, very strong Puerto Rican. Too many people make fun of the Puerto Ricans. Very fine people. Lots of class. We got José Torres, Mario Procaccino . . .

TANDY: All right, I'll go along with you for a second. You're God. Why would you be sweeping up, a lowly job like that?

ATTENDANT: It's therapeutic. I like it. It's easy on the nerves.

TANDY: God . . . A Puerto Rican steambath attendant. That'll be the day.

ATTENDANT: Look, I'll tell you what, fella. You say I'm not God. All right. You got it. I'm not God. Fabulous. You got what you want. (*Pointing to* BIEBERMAN) *He's* God.

OLDTIMER: He ain't God. He's a slob.

BIEBERMAN: Everything doesn't pay off in cleanliness. There are other virtues.

OLDTIMER: You stink to the high heavens.

TWO YOUNG MEN: We've reached the conclusion that you're being much too tough on him.

OLDTIMER: Don't you two ever split up?

TWO YOUNG MEN (*Seductively*): Make us an offer.

ATTENDANT: Mister, just don't bug me. All right? I got a lot on my mind.

TANDY: There's another one. God talking slang. How can I go along with that?

ATTENDANT: I talk any way I want, man. The Lord speaks in funny ways. Remember that. You want to discuss the relativity of mass, the Lorentz Transformation, galactic intelligence, I'll give you that, too. Just don't bug me. All right? Don't be no wise ass.

TANDY: That was more like it. You had me going there for a second. I respect anyone who really knows something, my work being as transitory as it is. It's when you talk dirty . . .

ATTENDANT: The way I talk, the way I talk . . . Don't you see that's just a little blink of an eye in terms of the universe, the job I got to do? The diameter of an electron is one ten-trillionth of an inch. And you're telling me I shouldn't talk dirty. Let me talk the way I want. Let me relax a little.

TANDY: I can't see it. You're not God.

ATTENDANT: You can't see it? Don't see it. I got things to do.

(*Approaches console screen again*)

All right, give that girl on the bus a run on her body stocking. I want to close up that branch of Schrafft's . . . And send up a bacon-and-lettuce-and-tomato sandwich, hold the mayo. You burn the toast, I'll smite you down with my terrible swift sword.

(*Leaves the console*)

TANDY: I still don't buy it. That could be an ordinary TV screen. You could have been watching *Laugh-In*.

ATTENDANT: *Laugh-In?* (*Goes over to console*) Cancel *Laugh-In.* You still want to fool around?

TANDY: I don't watch *Laugh-In.* Only thing I watch on TV is pro football. Gets better every year. Look, you're asking me to buy a whole helluva lot. You're challenging every one of my beliefs.

ATTENDANT: You think I care about your beliefs? With the job I got on my mind?

TANDY: You care. I may be one man, but there exists within me the seed of all mankind.

ATTENDANT: Very good. I'm going to give you a ninety on that.

TANDY: I used to tell that to my art-appreciation students over at the Police Academy.

ATTENDANT: Nice bunch of boys.

TANDY: You mean to tell me that you control every action on earth by means of that monitor over there? Every sneeze, every headache, every time a guy cuts himself? How can you possibly do so much?

ATTENDANT: I go very fast. You got to move like crazy. You can't stop and talk to every schmuck who comes along . . .

(GOTTLIEB, *attendant's assistant, comes in with a tray*)

GOTTLIEB: Your BLT down, sir.

ATTENDANT: Thank you. What do I owe you for that?

GOTTLIEB: Are you kidding, sire?

ATTENDANT: Just thought I'd ask. You don't have to get snotty about it.

(GOTTLIEB *goes off.* ATTENDANT *eats*)

TANDY: I don't know. It's awfully hard to accept. I've heard of having your faith tested, but this is ridiculous.

ATTENDANT (*Chewing BLT*): And who said you could speak while I was eating?

TANDY: All right. I'm sorry. I beg your pardon. One minute you're casual, the next you're formal. How can I keep up with you?

ATTENDANT: Changeable, mysterious, infinite, unfathomable. That's my style . . .

TANDY: Yeah—except that you're not God.

ATTENDANT: That's the conclusion you reached after all the time I spent with you? I'll tell you right now you're getting me roped off. I get roped off, watch out. Then you're really in trouble. (*Pulling himself together*) All right. I'll tell you what. You say I'm not God, right?

TANDY: Right.

ATTENDANT (*Pulling out deck of cards, and spreading them, like fan*): All right. Pick a card, any card.

TANDY: What's that gonna prove?

ATTENDANT: Go ahead, just do what I'm tellin' you. You'll see.

(TANDY *picks card*)

You look at it?

TANDY: Yes.

ATTENDANT (*Squinting eyes*): Okay . . . you got the . . . King of Hearts . . . Right?

(BROKER, *most nervous of all characters, applauds*)

TANDY: All right. You did it. So what?

ATTENDANT: So there y'are.

TANDY: There I am what? You do a simple card trick that any kid can do—a retarded kid can do—and I'm supposed to think you're God.

ATTENDANT: Can you do it?

TANDY: No, I can't do it. I can't even deal a hand of black-jack. But there are hundreds of guys who can do that trick. In every village and hamlet in the country. What the hell does that prove?

ATTENDANT: Not in the hamlets. It's not that easy. In the villages, maybe, but not in the hamlets. All right, I show you a trick that's not as easy as it seems, you won't buy it. Fair enough. You're pushing me to the wall. I'm not saying a word. Now, check my pants. And easy on the corporeal contact.

(TANDY *begrudgingly does so*)

Anything in there?

TANDY: There's nothing in there.

ATTENDANT (*With a flourish*): Now . . . (*Pulls out a long multi-colored scarf*) How's that? (*Drapes it over* MEREDITH *as a shawl*)

TANDY: I've seen it about a dozen times.

ATTENDANT: Where?

TANDY: On the Sullivan Show. These Slavic guys come over
here and do that trick. On a bicycle. Someone tells
them they can come over here and clean up. Sullivan's
the only one who'll give them a break. They make a
few bucks, you never hear from them again. They go
right back to those Slavic countries. Look, I'm sorry. I
don't know quite how to say this, but you are not even
putting a *dent* in me. What kind of second-rate horse-
shit is this?

ATTENDANT (*Gesturing as though he is pulling a knife out
of his chest*): Madre de Dios. You hurt my feelings
just now, you know that, don't you?

TANDY: There's a perfect example. God with his feelings
hurt. Ridiculous.

ATTENDANT: My feelings are not supposed to get hurt?
Once in a while? All right. Now I'm really going to
give you one. (*Calling into the wings*) Gottlieb.

>   (ASSISTANT *runs out with a footlocker
>   kept shut by a huge padlock. Sets it down*)

Thanks, Gottlieb, I won't forget this. (*To* TANDY) All
right. Check the lock.

TANDY (*Following instructions*): I checked it.

ATTENDANT: Is it strong?

TANDY: Very strong, very powerful. Big deal.

ATTENDANT: All right. Observez-vous.

> (GOTTLIEB *ties his hands behind him.* HE *kneels down and, with his teeth, sawing away like a bulldog, chews and chews and finally springs the lock.* GOTTLIEB *has been doing an accompanying song-and-dance routine, neatly timed, as though they have been through this many times before. With lock in his teeth, arms upraised, like a trapeze man,* ATTENDANT *acknowledges applause.* GOTTLIEB *throws a few ribbons of confetti over his head*)

Voilà!

TANDY: It was okay, I admit. It was a little better than the others. At least you're showing me a little something. Look, I don't know how to get this across to you, but you are not reaching me with this stuff. Maybe I'm crazy. (*To* STEAMBATH PEOPLE, *who are visible through the haze now*) Are you people impressed?

OLDTIMER: Only one fella I know could do that, fella named Radio. Sneaky little bugger, ran into him in New Guinea. Used to go crazy over radios. If you were carrying one, he'd figure out a way to get it away from you. Old Radio could have picked that lock with his teeth, no question about it . . .

ATTENDANT: There y'are. You heard what the man said. Only one other fellow could've pulled off that stunt. Radio.

TANDY: Wonderful. Look, I can't help it. Sue me. I'm not moved. If you had made one interesting intellectual assault on my mind, maybe that would do it.

ATTENDANT: De gustibus non est disputandum.

TANDY: That's it? That's the intellectual assault? Freshman English?

ATTENDANT: Have you ever really pondered it? Savored it? Rolled it around on your tongue and really tasted of its fruit?

TANDY: That's right. I have. And it's nothing. It's garbage. It's not the kind of insight to make the senses reel.

ATTENDANT (*Gathering others about him*): Consider the mind, an independent substance implanted within the soul and incapable of being destroyed . . . The City of Satan, whatever its artifices in art, war, or philosophy, was essentially corrupt and impious, its joy but a comic mask and its beauty the whitening of a sepulchre. It stood condemned before man's better conscience by its vanity, cruelty, and secret misery, by its ignorance of all that it truly behooved a man to know who was destined to immortality . . . Or how about this one: "A little philosophy inclineth man's mind to atheism, but depth in philosophy bringeth men's minds about to religion."

TANDY: Much better. Maybe I could even chew on some of that. But you still haven't got me. All I can see is a fairly interesting guy. For a Puerto Rican. If I ran into you at a bar—a Puerto Rican bar—maybe we could kick around a few ideas. All I'm saying is I don't see God yet. Where's God?

ATTENDANT: You don't see God, huh? Boy, you're some pistol. All right, here comes a little number that is going to make your head swim. You happen to be in luck, fella, because you caught me at cocktail time and I'm dry as a bone. Gottlieb . . . Now you watch this carefully . . .

(GOTTLIEB *emerges with tray of drinks*)

How many drinks you estimate are on that tray?

TANDY: Ten . . .

(ATTENDANT *begins to knock them off, one at a time*)

. . . and you don't even have to bother drinking them, because I can name you two lushes out there on

Eighth Avenue who can do the same thing . . . I mean, what is this . . . it's not even as good as the trunk. You might have snapped off a few teeth on that one . . . but this cheap, trivial, broken-down, ninth-rate . . .

(*As* HE *speaks,* GOTTLIEB *returns, struggling to bring in an enormous whiskey sour, one that towers above* TANDY'*s head.* TANDY *is thunderstruck*)

Are you *mad?*

ATTENDANT: Un momento.

(HE *leaps to top tier of column, sits opposite rim of glass, pulls out a straw and takes a sip*)

Delicious. That son of a bitch makes some drink.

(ATTENDANT *finishes up with a flourish, leaps down*)

All right, what have you got to say to that, baby? Incidentally, you like the cherry, go ahead, don't be embarrassed . . .

TANDY: It was pretty good. All right. I take that back. Fair is fair. It was great. My hat goes off to you. It was really remarkable. I figure the odds were about fifty to one against. I hardly know how to say this next thing, but I'm still not buying it. The God routine.

ATTENDANT: You're still not buying it?

TANDY: No sir. The fact that I just said "sir" will give you an indication that I'm really impressed. You got a lot going for you. But I'm not really there yet. If I said I bought the whole thing you'd know I wasn't being straight. It would be an injustice of a kind. A real sell-out.

ATTENDANT: So then you still don't buy it.

TANDY: No sir.

ATTENDANT: You really making me work, boy. All right. I have but one choice, my son. (*Gestures*) Shazam . . .

> (*Stage, theatre, suddenly fill with deafening organ music, churchlike, ancient, soaring, almost unbearable. Theatre then fills with angels or other miraculous and heavenly effects.* ATTENDANT *stands majestically, his head crowned with celestial light.* HE *ascends to highest tier in steambath. Music is deafening in its churchlike call to the divinity. Voice of* ATTENDANT, *magnified a hundredfold, similar to that of Cecil B. DeMille, booms out*)

ATTENDANT'S VOICE: ASCRIBE UNTO THE LORD
    YE KINDREDS OF THE PEOPLES . . .
    ASCRIBE UNTO THE LORD

GLORY AND STRENGTH . . .
ASCRIBE UNTO THE LORD
THE GLORY DUE UNTO HIS NAME
BRING AN OFFERING
AND COME UNTO HIS COURTS
OH, WORSHIP THE LORD
IN THE BEAUTY OF HOLINESS
TREMBLE BEFORE HIM
ALL THE EARTH . . .

(*One by one, the* STEAMBATH PEOPLE *drop to their knees.* TANDY *looks around, observes that* HE *is the only one standing.* HE *shrugs, goes to one knee*)

AS THE CURTAIN DESCENDS

"You don't think?" murmurs MEREDITH (Annie
Rachel), and TANDY (Anthony Perkins)
completes her thought, *"We're dead? Is that
what you were going to say? That's what I was
going to say. That's what we are."*

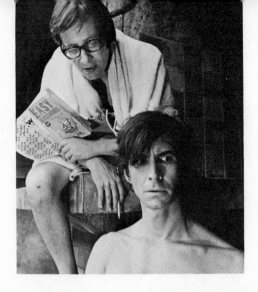

"What's a six-letter word that means little red spikes of corn?" BIEBERMAN (Marvin Lichterman) asks the bewildered TANDY.

"Boy, this is some place!" exclaims TANDY after being serenaded by the two delicate YOUNG MEN (Jere Admire and Teno Pollick).

TANDY cuts in on the BROKER's (Mitchell Jason) monologue: *"I don't want to hurt your feelings or anything, but I'm really not that interested in your bowel movements . . ."*

MEREDITH takes a shower.

Morty, the steambath ATTENDANT (Hector Elizondo), instructs his console to *"Give that girl on the bus a run in her body stocking."*

The OLDTIMER (Conrad Bain) observes,
*"Toughest son of a bitch I ever knew used to
dress up like Carmen Miranda."*

All the action takes place in a steamroom, with
jets of steam billowing from pipes set in the
floor upstage and people appearing and
disappearing in the haze.

In the last of a series of attempts to prove that he is God, Morty downs an enormous whiskey sour. . .

The group is impressed but not convinced and
so—to the sound of deafening organ music—the
ATTENDANT appears transfigured, and they all
kneel before him.

TANDY tries to throttle GOTTLIEB (Gabor Morea) to force him to betray his Lord.

When the OLDTIMER's hour strikes, he hitches himself up with great dignity, and executes a bum's dance before proudly walking out through the door.

"I got to talk to you about getting out of here," TANDY explains, *"I don't belong here, I don't need this,"* and there is a light in Morty's eye as he replies, *"You know what I don't need? Right now? Aggravation."*

PEOPLE *are all lying around, exhausted, as though after a heavy night-long bacchanal*

(BROKER *comes skipping in with a rope*)

BROKER (*To* TANDY): You ought to try this . . . Really gets the weight off you . . . Look in the mirror sometime while you're doing it. Everything moves. The stuff way inside—where you have the real weight—that's moving too . . . (*Stops jumping*) How much do you weigh? . . .

TANDY: Me? Around 190 . . . 195 . . . somewhere in there . . .

BROKER: I'm 179 myself. I'd like to lose around ten, twelve pounds. Twelve pounds I'd feel like a tiger . . . (*Grabbing some flesh about his waist*) I got to lose it around here—that's where it's rough . . . 'specially when you get around my age . . .

TANDY: That's right . . .

BROKER: One hundred sixty-eight. That's my perfect weight. You should see me at 168. Never seen anything like it . . .

TANDY: I bet you look great . . .

BROKER: I do. I get up in the middle, high seventies, forget
it. It's all gone . . . You want to hear something
else . . .

TANDY: Shoot.

BROKER: When I'm 168, I get a beautiful bowel movement
. . . How about you. You pretty regular?

TANDY: I don't want to hurt your feelings or anything, but
I'm really not that interested in your bowel movements . . .

BROKER: I can see that . . . Sorry if I was presumptuous . . .

TANDY: Perfectly all right . . .

BROKER: I once bought a stock at 168—my exact weight
. . . Fellow who recommended it said this is a stock
you don't worry about. It goes off, for argument's sake,
ten, twenty, fifty points, I don't care if it goes off a
hundred points . . . you don't worry about this stock.
So I hold it. And it *does* go off ten, twenty, over a
hundred points. The stock is now selling at a fast ten
points. So I call the guy. It's down to ten, I say. When
do I start worrying? "Never," he says. He just wasn't a
worrier. I lost every penny . . . Shows you . . . go trust
people . . . I should've stuck to ferns . . .

TANDY: Ferns?

BROKER: That's right. I was in the fern game for a while. A lot of people go in for ferns, you'd be surprised. I was cleaning up. But I couldn't take the social pressure . . . Guy at a party'd ask me what do you do, I'd say I'm in ferns . . . How do you think that made me feel?

OLDTIMER: Turn off that TV set . . .

BROKER: I had to get out . . .

BIEBERMAN: I'm watching a wonderful forties' movie. And it's down very low.

OLDTIMER: Turn it off, I tell you. I'm trying to catch a quick snooze. Turn it off or I'll come up there and kick you in the bazanzas . . .

BIEBERMAN: What are they?

OLDTIMER: Never mind. You'll find out fast enough if I kick you there.

BIEBERMAN: Anti-Semite.

OLDTIMER: I'm an anti-stinkite. That's what *you* got to worry about. Now turn it off, I tell you . . .

BIEBERMAN (*Always a little bitter, angry when* HE *speaks, spitting the words out deliberately*): I suppose it never occurred to you that every smile, every whisper, every puff of a cigarette taken by my generation was inspired by the forties' movie. That my generation wouldn't know how to mix a drink, drive a car, kiss a girl, straighten a tie—if it weren't for Linda Darnell and George Brent . . . That the sole reason for my generation's awkward floundering in the darkness is that Zachary Scott is gone . . . and I assure you that Dennis Hopper is no substitute . . .

OLDTIMER: I'll tell you what your generation needs. A movie that instructs you on how to smell like a human being. You can star in it. (*To* TANDY) How can he even see the screen with all this steam . . .

BIEBERMAN: When it gets too dense I smear it off with a corner of my jockey shorts . . .

OLDTIMER: I spent four years in the Philippines I never ran into a slob like that. (*Suddenly clutches at his chest, as though having a heart attack, then realizes this is impossible and gestures as if to say "The hell with it"*)

TANDY: C'mon, you guys, knock it off. You're supposed to be dead. Act like it.

MEREDITH: It's wonderful the way they listen to you.

TANDY: It's probably that time I spent with the cops. It really changes you. Even when you're in the art department. One day they invited me on an assault case and these two detectives, kidding around, threw me out on a fire escape with this huge transvestite—had arms like a boilermaker. Anyway, we're on the thirty-fifth floor, we start grappling with each other, and I figure it's either me or it. So I bit him in the ear. Well, it must have turned him on because all of a sudden he confesses that he electrocuted a hippy in Vermont. Well, I told him I was kidding around, I wasn't a real dick, but he just kept confessing and I kept biting and finally they hauled us both back through the window and booked him on the Vermont thing and me on a morals charge—I'm just kidding . . . I finally had to get out of the cops, it was a terrible place . . . there *was* one thing—I could always run up a tab at the Automat . . .

MEREDITH: Oh, my God . . .

TANDY: What's wrong?

MEREDITH: I just remembered. I haven't paid my Bloomingdale's bill.

TANDY: When was it due?

MEREDITH: Last Monday . . . now they'll probably send me one of those thin gray envelopes . . . You have no idea how much I hate those envelopes . . .

TANDY: But it's ridiculous. You can't pay your bills now. The store will understand.

MEREDITH: Bloomingdale's! I don't know why they insist on making you feel so terrible. Any other store—Saks, Bendel's—if you don't pay your bill they assume you're in Acapulco. Not Bloomingdale's. Right for the throat. "In ten days if you have not paid your bill, we are cutting off your charge account and telling your parents, friends, and the principal of the first school you attended . . ."

TANDY: Look, obviously none of this has sunk in. We're in big trouble. We could be stuck in this lousy steambath forever. You're sitting around talking Bloomingdale's. You saw that Puerto Rican guy . . . He wasn't kidding around . . .

MEREDITH: That was fun.

TANDY: What do you mean?

MEREDITH: The part where we got down on our knees. We used to do that at Marymount every morning, first thing, and it was freezing. It was fun getting down on a nice warm floor for a change . . .

TANDY: It wasn't any fun for me. I got to get out of here. I got all this Charlemagne research to do. There's going to be a whole Charlemagne revival, I can tell. Books, movies, musical comedies. Dolls—that's right. Little Charlemagne dolls. And I'll be left out of it. Where is that guy? I'm going to take another shot at him.

(*Disappears for the moment in haze*)

BIEBERMAN: Anyone have some pimple lotion . . .

OLDTIMER: There he goes again, the cocksucker . . .

BIEBERMAN: Well, can I control my complexion, can I?

OLDTIMER: Of course you can. Ever hear of cutting down on malteds?

BIEBERMAN: I'll never cut down on malteds, never.

OLDTIMER: Well, then, don't come to me with your pimples, you stupid bastard.

BIEBERMAN: Malteds are the marijuana of my generation.

OLDTIMER: Your generation . . . what the hell generation is that?

BIEBERMAN: It went by very quickly . . . It was Dolf Camilli, Dane Clark, Uncle Don, Ducky Medwick and out . . .

OLDTIMER: Sounds like a real bunch of winners.

BIEBERMAN: We produced Norman Podhoretz.

OLDTIMER: Congratulations . . . (*To the* BROKER) Who the fuck is Norman Podhoretz?

BROKER: Probably some wealthy bastard who made it when you could keep it.

TANDY (*Entering*): We're all set.

MEREDITH: What's up?

TANDY: I've got a whole bunch of carpet tacks.

MEREDITH: Wow. Where did you get them?

TANDY: They got an old carpet rolled up back there.

MEREDITH: What good'll they do?

TANDY: Plenty. Don't undersell them. I once saw a guy with only a handful of carpet tacks get the best of two armed cops.

MEREDITH: That's remarkable, overpowering two policemen that way.

TANDY: That's right. Where is that guy. Listen, we get out, I'd like you to see my apartment. I've got big steel bars on the windows—I had a few robberies—but I've got the bars painted in psychedelic colors. I've got huge double security locks—they're painted in psychedelic colors, too. Burglar alarm—same deal.

MEREDITH: I'd love to see your apartment.

TANDY: I'd like you to see it. It's not a horny thing. I won't jump on you or anything.

MEREDITH: Oh, I know that . . .

TANDY: Well, as a matter of fact, it *is* a partially horny thing. You're a very good-looking girl . . . but I'm also proud of the apartment.

MEREDITH: Don't you have a girl friend?

TANDY: Oh yes, I've got an ex-wife, a mistress, a mother . . . I'm covered on all sides. Now I just need a girl . . .

MEREDITH: I understand. You just want someone totally uncomplicated.

TANDY: That's right.

MEREDITH: It's only fair to tell you that I can only sleep with one man at a time. If I slept with you I might reach across in the middle of the night and think I was stroking Raymondo . . .

TANDY: Raymondo? Listen, don't worry about it. I just want you to see my place sometime . . . Listen, you and your roommate don't . . . I mean . . . together.

MEREDITH: Make scenes? . . . Oh no . . . we don't do that.

TANDY: I hope you don't take offense . . . I was just checking.

MEREDITH: We don't any more, that is. We did take a mescaline trip recently with one of my stockbroker friends. It didn't work out. It turned into a sort of business trip.

TANDY: Well, look, I don't need that right now. I got my hands full the way it is . . . It's just that when you work with the cops you see a lot of crazy things, you get ideas. You should go out on a few homicides. You should see what incensed Mexicans do to their common-law wives when they step out of line. Believe me, you'd never want to be a Mexican common-law wife.

MEREDITH: Oh, I don't know. I hear Cuernavaca's beautiful.

OLDTIMER (*To* BROKER): Toughest son of a bitch I ever knew used to dress up like Carmen Miranda. They found him floating five kilometers outside Hamburg Harbor . . . all those bananas bobbing in the water.

(ATTENDANT *enters,* GOTTLIEB *along with him*)

ATTENDANT: All right, everybody, campfire time. Gottlieb, give out the Mounds bars.

(GOTTLIEB *distributes candy bars to* STEAM-BATH INHABITANTS, *who gather round an improvised campfire site*)

MEREDITH (*Accepting a candy bar*): Oh, I love these . . .

TANDY (*Calling* ATTENDANT *aside*): Listen, I want to talk to you about getting out of here. I got a lot of deals going on the outside, a lot of things to clear up. I don't know if you know anything about Charlemagne . . .

ATTENDANT: The Puerto Rican?

TANDY: Cute. Listen, I haven't mentioned it yet, but I want you to know that was very impressive stuff you did, drinking all that stuff, those lights . . . very good . . .

ATTENDANT: I saw you on your knees.

TANDY: One knee. I just went down on one knee . . . Maybe that's half-assed, I don't know. Maybe a straight solid guy—a Henry Cabot Lodge—would have either given you both knees or said the hell with it . . . I don't know. I figured you run the place I'll throw you one knee. A little respect. Meanwhile, I got to talk to you about getting out of here. I don't belong here, I don't need this.

ATTENDANT: You know what I don't need? Right now? Aggravation.

TANDY: God, aggravated. There's another hot one.

ATTENDANT: Listen, if you're God, the name of the game is aggravation. Anyway, I don't want to hear anymore.

You say another word, baby, I'll become wrathful and vengeance-seeking.

(*Gestures to* BROKER *to begin*)

BROKER: For twenty years I was mad at my partner.

ATTENDANT: Once upon a time . . .

BROKER: Excuse me . . . Once upon a time for twenty years I was mad at my partner.

ATTENDANT: Hold it a second. Any broads in this story?

BROKER: No.

ATTENDANT: Gottlieb, you want to stay?

(GOTTLIEB *shrugs*)

He likes serious stuff, too, otherwise I wouldn't keep him around. But once in a while he likes to hear about broads. Go ahead . . .

BROKER: We were partners for twenty years. Somehow he had everything—a glass house, schnauzer dogs, cuff links you should have seen the size of them . . . And I'm living in three rooms in Washington Heights. It was eating at me. I figure we're partners. How come I don't have a glass house and schnauzer dogs. So one day I went to visit him in his house and I put it to him. He listens to my complaints, goes inside, and comes out with a check for eight hundred dollars. Well, I couldn't figure out that check. How did he come up with that figure? But amazingly, I wasn't angry. After all, eight hundred was eight hundred. So I went outside and sat on the golf course. I never liked to play, but I do like to sit on a golf course. And that's how they found me, sitting on a director's chair, right near the fourth hole, with the eight-hundred-dollar check in my lap and my head thrown back like this. (HE *demonstrates, throwing back his head, opening his mouth wide and baring his teeth grotesquely*) They all came back and when they saw me, they all made that face too, that same face. They all threw back their heads and opened their mouths and made the same dead face I had. (HE *demonstrates again*)

ATTENDANT: It's going to be hard to give you a ninety on that one.

MEREDITH: I thought it was fascinating. I wonder why they wanted to make that face. (SHE *tries it*)

OLDTIMER: That's easy. They wanted to taste a little death without really being dead.

MEREDITH: Oh, I see. Gee, this is good. It's just like Camp Aurora. Who's next?

TWO YOUNG MEN: We both hung ourselves for love of the same boy—a swing dancer in the national company of *Zorba*.

We never realized we could love someone that . . .
indifferent . . . we loved the way he moved . . . the
rough carving of his arms . . . the way the veins were
printed on them.
We'd go to the all-night skating rinks . . . And then,
unaccountably, he simply left the show—and went
back to school in North Carolina.
Totally unmarked by us—as though we'd been a slight
change in the direction of the wind.
Neither of us meant a thing to him . . .
. . . We were no more than a pair of cats that crossed
his path in a strange village and slowed his walk for
a moment.
He was beautiful.

ATTENDANT: Tell you the truth, I never went in very much
for fag stories.

MEREDITH: I thought it was very touching.

ATTENDANT: I'm a sympathizer . . . but they don't really
satisfy me.

TWO YOUNG MEN: Well, you wrote it.

ATTENDANT: That's true. But you know how it is when
you're a writer. You write some stuff you don't like.
Who's got a good one?

TANDY: This is very unjust. You've obviously set this thing
up for your own amusement.

ATTENDANT: And you don't like that. I'm not allowed to
have a few laughs. Listen, you been giving me a hard
time ever since you come in here . . . You show up . . .
you don't like it . . . you hand me this Charlemagne
routine . . . I'm going to do a bad thing to you now.

TANDY (*Alarmed*): What's that? I admit I'm frightened.
What are you going to do? (*Looks at second door*)
You're not going to put me in there, are you?

ATTENDANT: No. (*Points to* OLDTIMER) I'm putting him
in there. (*To* TANDY) You come in here . . . you're
looking for fair, reasonable . . . Where'd you get that
from? Old man . . .

OLDTIMER (*Rising*): My time, eh?

ATTENDANT: That's right, baby.

OLDTIMER: Well, that's okay. I done everything. I once
had a pair of perfectly matched wooden-legged
frauleins powder me up from head to toe and dress
me up in silk drawers. I run up against a Greek
sailor walking around for thirty years with a lump on
his chest he took to be a natural growth. Turned out
to be the unborn fetus of a twin brother he'd spent all
his life hankering for. I seen most everything. I dipped
my beak in Madrid, Spain; Calcutta, India; Leningrad,
Russia, and I never once worried about them poisoning
the water. I had myself the fifth-richest woman in
Sydney, Australia, genuine duchess she was, all dressed

up in a tiger suit; by the time I finished with her I had them stripes going the wrong way. I played a pretty good trumpet. I had to face the fact that I was no Harry James, but then again, Sir Harry couldn't go in there and break up a Polish wedding the way I could. I talked back to the biggest guys. Didn't bother me. I didn't care if it was me way down in the valley, hollering up at Mount Zion. I'd holler up some terrific retorts. You're not going to show me anything I haven't seen. I paid my dues. (*Starts to go*) And I'll tell you something else. If there's anything in there kicks me, you watch and see if I don't bite.

> (HE *hitches himself up with great dignity and does a sailor's dance, then a proud old-man's walk into the grated room*)

ATTENDANT: Old man had a lot of balls.

TANDY: Damn right. (*To* ATTENDANT) Listen, I was the wise guy. Why didn't you send me in there?

ATTENDANT: That's direct. I don't work that way. I always put a little spin on the ball. Okay. This is the last one. I want live actors this time.

> (*A cheap lower-class bar is set up—or at least the skeletal representation of one.* TWO MEN *stand on opposite sides of the bar. One is a* LONGSHOREMAN; *the other is* GOTTLIEB, *who plays the part of a bartender for this scene.*)

LONGSHOREMAN (*Setting the scene for the* ATTENDANT):
A longshoreman's bar in Astoria, Queens.

(ATTENDANT *gestures for him to proceed*)

LONGSHOREMAN: We ought to take our six toughest guys—
and the Russians—they take their six toughest guys.
Send 'em into a forest—they can have it over there if
they want. And the guys that walk out of that forest—
that's it.

GOTTLIEB (*Tending bar*): Those Commies would have to
shut up.

LONGSHOREMAN: Oh, the Russians are all right. If you ask
me, they can build a machine as good as America. But
fortunately for us, they lack the human people to
operate that machine.

GOTTLIEB: You better believe it.

> (*A couple enters the bar. The* MAN *is in a
> wheelchair; his legs, braced, are apparently
> useless.* HE *wears steel-rimmed glasses and
> his neck, too, is coiled in a brace, as though
> he has been in a whiplash accident. Very
> eerie.* HE *is with a young, pretty girl in a
> short skirt. The* GIRL *puts a quarter in the
> jukebox—some rock music begins. The*
> GIRL *starts to dance—in the modern style—
> quite seductively, in front of the wheel-*

chaired fellow. The FELLOW *in the chair
snaps his fingers and responds to the music
to the best of his abilities*)

GOTTLIEB (*Referring to couple*): Hey . . .

LONGSHOREMAN: Yeah . . .

GOTTLIEB: Ever seen anything like that?

LONGSHOREMAN: No, I never have.

(*They watch the couple awhile*)

LONGSHOREMAN: Watch this. (*He approaches* COUPLE,
speaks to GIRL) Say, miss . . .

GIRL DANCER: Yes . . .

LONGSHOREMAN (*Referring to fellow in chair*): All systems
are not go . . .

GIRL DANCER (*Still dancing*): I don't follow you . . .

LONGSHOREMAN: You know . . . the astronauts . . . all systems are not go. Wouldn't you rather move around
with a guy whose systems are all à go-go?

WHEELCHAIRED MAN (*Talking through a throat box, as
though the victim of a tracheotomy*): Why are you
harassing us? We were behaving peaceably.

LONGSHOREMAN: I hadn't noticed. (HE *grabs* GIRL) C'mon, baby, let's move around a little . . . (GIRL *moves half-heartedly*)

WHEELCHAIRED MAN: You've just made a serious mistake, fella.

LONGSHOREMAN: That right?

WHEELCHAIRED MAN: That's right. First of all . . . (HE *switches off throat box and speaks in a normal tone*) I don't really speak that way. (*Twirls off whiplash collar*) Second of all, I don't wear this . . . Third of all . . . (*Getting to his feet and kicking off braces*) I don't need these. Last but not least . . . (*Whipping off his shirt to show a well-muscled frame and huge championship belt*) . . . silver-belt karate, the highest karate level of all . . . (*With three quick moves,* HE *wipes out* LONGSHOREMAN, *who falls to the floor. At a certain point in the* WHEELCHAIRED MAN'S *metamorphosis, it has become apparent that* HE *is* BIEBERMAN)

ATTENDANT (*Delighted at the discovery*): Hey! Bieberman! . . . You wipe him out and then you and the chick leave . . .

BIEBERMAN: That's right.

ATTENDANT: How many times you get away with that stunt?

BIEBERMAN: Twenty-five times. Sarah and I started to do it every Friday night, as a form of social involvement, a means of smoking out society's predators . . .

ATTENDANT: But you kept getting away with it. I forget, what are you doing here?

BIEBERMAN: An Arab at the 92nd Street YMHA dropped a 200-pound barbell on my neck.

ATTENDANT: That's right. And don't you forget it. . . . All right, everybody, that does it . . . You told some pretty good stuff, but we got to make room for the next crowd. (*Gesturing toward second door*) . . . Everybody in there . . . We enjoyed having you, sincerely.

BROKER: All this exercise—the steam—what good did it do?

ATTENDANT: What are you complaining about—you're in the best shape of your life . . .

BROKER: That's true. Well, I'll go first. I been finished for a long time. (*Hesitates*) Years ago, when you wound up your steambath, there'd be a man outside selling pumpernickel and pickled fish . . .

ATTENDANT: I'll send some in . . . don't worry . . . Now let's go . . . chop-chop . . .

(BROKER *goes through the door*)

1ST YOUNG MAN: Do I look all right?

2ND YOUNG MAN: You look great. It'll be a relief to get out of all that steam.

1ST YOUNG MAN: It's destroyed your hair. Maybe Ralph will be in there.

2ND YOUNG MAN: Ralph? From Amagansett?

1ST YOUNG MAN: He *was* tacky.

(THEY *go through the door*)

BIEBERMAN (*To* MEREDITH): Goodbye. My generation's out of style—I know that—but you'll never know the thrill of having belonged to it. (*Starting through grated door*) John Hodiak—hold on, I'll be right with you . . .

(HE *goes through*)

ATTENDANT (*Hollering after departed group*): And if I find any candy wrappers I'll send Gottlieb in there to kick your ass.

(*Only* TANDY *and* MEREDITH *remain*)

TANDY: Kick your ass, kick your ass . . . I'm supposed to respect that? . . . Where's the grandeur? . . . the majesty? . . .

ATTENDANT: I'm saving that for the next group that's coming in. I hear they got some terrific broads. They're single. Bunch of nurses. They fell from a cable car . . . I'm going to hit them with all this grandeur and majesty . . .

> (*Goes over to console, which appears in the mist*)

Start a new rock and roll group called Grandeur and Majesty . . .

> (*Console blips back its response. To* MERE-DITH)

You goin', lady?

MEREDITH (*Hesitating*): Well, as I was telling Mr. Tandy, I've only recently had my first orgasm . . . and I haven't paid my Bloomingdale's bill. I've never been to Nassau in the Bahamas . . .

ATTENDANT: First orgasm . . . good-looking girl like you . . . Must have been a slip-up. Maybe you been having them all along and didn't realize it . . . All right, let's go, you two . . . I got a lot of cleaning up to do . . .

TANDY: I told you I'm not accepting this.

ATTENDANT: You want me to get rough?

TANDY: How would you like it if you were in the middle of a great Chinese restaurant . . . you've had your spare-ribs, a little soup—you're working up a terrific appetite and bam! You're thrown out of the restaurant. You never get to enjoy the Won Shih pancakes.

ATTENDANT: I can get any kind of food I want up here . . . except lox. The lox is lousy, pre-sliced . . . the kind you get in those German delicatessens . . . I can't get any fresh lox . . . I don't know why that is . . .

TANDY: It's like a guy about to have some terrific operation. The odds against him surviving are ridiculous, Newton High School against the Kansas City Chiefs. They're working on his eyes, ears, nose, throat, and brains. A whole squadron of doctors is flown in from the Caucasus where they have all these new Caucasus techniques. He's hanging by a hair—and miracle of miracles, he makes it. Gets back on his feet, says goodbye to the doctors, goes home, and gets killed by a junkie outside of Toots Shor's . . . That's the kind of thing you want me to accept.

ATTENDANT: That's a pretty good one. (*Takes a note on it*) I'm gonna use that . . . Yes, come to think of it, that is the kind of thing I want you to accept.

TANDY: Well, I can't. I worked too hard to get where I am . . . You know about Wendy Tandy, my ex-wife . . .

ATTENDANT: Good-looking broad, I know about her . . .

TANDY: That stunt she pulled?

ATTENDANT: That was a good one . . . Gottlieb, you got to
hear this . . .

(GOTTLIEB *comes over*)

TANDY (*More to* MEREDITH *than anyone*): She's an un-
faithful wife. Fine. You put up with it, you don't. I
did. Fair and square. So then we meet a retired hairdresser who has become an underground film-maker.
He shoots his film through those filters of teased hair
. . . it's a new technique. This is the guy Wendy falls
madly in love with. And she moves out—to live with
him. Fair and square. She prefers him, she's got him.
Swingin'. I'm getting along fine—got a few deals of
my own cooking—and all of a sudden I get an invita-
tion to go see a film that this hairdresser has put
Wendy in—down on Charles Street. And I find out—
in one of the Village papers—that what he's done is
make a huge blow-up—in one of the scenes—I don't
know how to say this—of her private parts. It's very
artistic, don't get me wrong . . . The audience thinks
it's a Soviet train station . . .

MEREDITH: God, I'd never do that. How did he get her to
do that. She must have really loved him.

ATTENDANT: Hey, Gottlieb, what did I tell you?

(GOTTLIEB *hangs his head.* HE's *shy*)

TANDY: Well, that makes me the supreme schmuck, cuckold, whatever you want to call it, everybody agreed? Half the city sitting in a theater, looking at my wife's box— sitting inside it, for Christ's sakes . . .

MEREDITH: For heaven's sake, what did you do?

TANDY: That's what I'm getting at. The old me would have come in with guns. I'm a very good shot—at under seven feet. There's a technique I learned over at the Academy. You run into a little room after this cornered guy and as you shoot you're supposed to start screaming (*Demonstrates*) YI, YI, YI, YI, YI, YI. That's in case you miss, you scare the shit out of him. But I finally figured, what the hell, it's nothing to do with me. She's that kind of a girl. I knock off this guy, the next one'll be Xeroxing her pussy all over Times Square. So I said the hell with it and I went to the movie.

MEREDITH: How was it?

TANDY: Not bad. As a director, the guy had some pretty good moves. It fell apart in the middle, but it was worth seeing. I sat in the balcony . . . But you see, I got past all that baloney. Out in the clear, after ten years . . . and I started getting straight in other areas, too. I got a wonderful, calm girl friend . . . We could be sitting at McGinnis' restaurant and Fidel Castro could walk in, She'd stay calm, low, even, maybe give

him a little smile. I love that. I never had it . . . And
then I forgave my mother . . .

MEREDITH: For what?

TANDY: I never liked the work she was doing. She ran a
chain of dancing schools in Appalachia. She'd talk
these starving families into taking mambo lessons . . .
very bitter woman. Anyway, I took her out of Appalachia, got her an apartment in White Plains, and I
like her now. She's seventy, and all that iron has
dropped out of her.

GOTTLIEB (*To* ATTENDANT): Any more sexy parts?

ATTENDANT: Shut up, Gottlieb. I think that's wonderful the
boy's nice to his mother. I didn't know that . . . (*To*
TANDY). What else you got? . . .

TANDY: I just kept ironing out all the wrinkles in my life.
The toughest thing, believe it or not, was leaving my
art-appreciation job over at the Police Academy. I
really thought the dicks would kill me if I left. They
didn't. They gave me a wonderful send-off party. They
hired a little combo—four convicted forgers—and
they ran some Danish art films they'd confiscated at
a Bar Mitzvah in Great Neck. And then at the end
my art students gave me a replica of Michelangelo's
David—seventy-five bucks over at Brentano's . . .
Only one fellow gave me any trouble, detective named
Flanders, said if I left he'd trail me all over the world,

any place I tried to hide—and hunt me down like a dog.

(DETECTIVE FLANDERS *appears, gun in hand*)

FLANDERS: Tandy . . .

TANDY (*Running*): Jesus . . .

ATTENDANT: You kidding? Don't worry about this guy.

(*Gestures and* FLANDERS' *gun turns to a milkshake*)

All right now, get in there.

(FLANDERS *goes through the door*)

TANDY: That was close.

MEREDITH: I'm glad he's on our side.

ATTENDANT: You see, I told you. And you said nasty things about me. You called me a bad guy . . .

TANDY: Anyway, you get the idea. I've gotten my whole life on the right track for the first time. I don't hate Wendy. I'm doing this wonderful work for brain-damaged welders. You ask the welders what they think of me. And I've got a marvelous new girl who's got this surprising body. You look at her face you just don't expect all that voluptuousness. You say to yourself, she's a little girl, a quiet little girl, comes from a nice family, where did these tits come from . . .

ATTENDANT: Hey, hey, there's a lady . . .

MEREDITH: Oh, that's all right. I don't mind tits. Knockers is the one I don't care for.

TANDY: All right, excuse me, but do you get the idea? I got everything bad swept out of the room. I'm closer than ever to my daughter. That trip to Vegas really brought us together. I'm doing work that I love. Warner Brothers saw the first hundred pages of my Charlemagne book and I understood they like it for Steve McQueen . . .

ATTENDANT: Twentieth is going to buy it . . . for Charlton Heston . . .

TANDY: Then you admit . . . you admit I'm getting out of here.

ATTENDANT: They're going to buy it from your estate . . .

TANDY: Look, I'm all clean and straight and honest. I got rid of all the garbage. Any crooked lines, I erased them and drew them straight . . . I don't hate anybody. I love a lot of people. I'm at the goddamned starting line. I'm ready to breathe clean air. I tore myself inside out to get to where I am—and I'm not taking up anybody's space. I'm ready to cook a little. Swing. What kind of fellow is that to snuff out?

ATTENDANT: A good fellow. But I'm snuffing him out anyway.

TANDY: Where's your compassion?

ATTENDANT: I do plenty of good things. Half the things I do are good, maybe even a little more, that's right, maybe even a little more. Nobody notices them. I never get any credit, but I do plenty of good things. I make trees, forests, soccer fields. I let hernias get better . . .

TANDY: But you'll wipe out a guy like me . . . and a lovely blonde girl like that . . .

MEREDITH: Oh, listen, the blonde part shouldn't enter into it, I can see that.

ATTENDANT: I let you go, I got to let the next guy go. Pretty soon nobody's dead. You'd have people coming out of your ears. Have you seen Istanbul lately? Downtown Istanbul? Los Angeles?

MEREDITH: I'd never live in L.A. I don't think there's one sincere person in the whole city.

ATTENDANT: Let me ask you something. While you were doing all those things, unloading your old lady, you know, straightening out your head, how did you feel?

TANDY: Good. Excited . . . it was like being in a whirlpool bath. An emotional whirlpool bath. It even made my body feel good; it got springy and toughened up . . .

ATTENDANT: There y'are. You felt good, you had a whirlpool bath . . . a springy body . . . Need I say more?

TANDY: You don't understand something. I probably never made it clear. This is very important to me. We're talking about my life. I'm not asking you for seats to a hockey game.

ATTENDANT (*Mocking*): It's very important to him. Nobody else is alive.

TANDY: Is there anything I can do for you?

ATTENDANT: You got to be kidding. *You* do something for *me?* What in the world would God want?

TANDY: A sacrifice? . . . burnt offering? . . .

ATTENDANT (*As though* HE *is finished with* TANDY): I got no time to fool around. I got a whole new crowd coming in.

TANDY: That's it. You're going through with this? Well, I'll tell you right now, if you're capable of wiping out a once-confused fellow who's now a completely straight and sweet guy, then I got no choice but to call you a prick. (*To* MEREDITH) I'm sorry.

MEREDITH: Oh, that's all right. You can say prick. Pecker is the one I don't care for.

ATTENDANT (*Astonished*): God? . . . Did I hear you correctly? . . . Can I believe my ears? . . . Blasphemy? . . .

TANDY: That's right. If you're capable of doing something like that. Taking a fellow to the very threshold of marvelous things, teasing him along and then aceing him out just when he's ready to scoop up one lousy drop of gravy—that is bad news, I'm sorry . . .

ATTENDANT: I'll tell you right now nobody ever called me that. That's bad, boy, that *is* low. Wowee . . . That's what I call sinning, baby. You're in real trouble now. You have put your foot in it this time, fella . . . You going to stick to what you called me? . . . that dirty name? . . . talking that way to God?

TANDY: Yeah, I'm going to stick to it . . . and you know why . . . because when I was in that Chinese restaurant . . . and I lost my breath, and I had no feelings, and I was numb and white, as white as a piece of typing paper, and I said over and over and over I don't want to die, I don't want to die, I don't want to die . . . and told you, in my way, how much I treasured every drop of life—you weren't impressed, you didn't hear a whisper of it . . .

ATTENDANT: That right, Gottlieb? Did he do that?

(GOTTLIEB *nods*)

TANDY: I thought you knew everything.

ATTENDANT: Almost everything. Once in a while there's an administrative error. Anyway, I did hear you. You came over a little weak, a little static thrown in there, but I heard you. That's why you're here. Otherwise . . . (*Pointing to grated door*) . . . you'd have gone straight in there . . .

TANDY: Then not everybody comes here . . .

ATTENDANT: Neurotics, freaks . . . (*contemptuously*) . . . those with stories to tell.

TANDY: How was mine?

ATTENDANT: Not bad. I heard worse.

TANDY: You were touched . . . You just won't admit it. (HE *advances, threateningly*) Now let me out of here.

ATTENDANT: You come near me, I'll send you back with cancer, then you'll know real trouble.

(TANDY *grabs* GOTTLIEB, *wrestles him to the floor, holding him around the neck, threatening him with his other hand*)

TANDY: All right, talk, and be quick about it. Otherwise, you get these carpet tacks right in your face. How do we get out of here?

ATTENDANT: You talk, Gottlieb, and I'll see to it that you never work again. What can he do with a lousy bunch of carpet tacks?

GOTTLIEB: I don't know. But I'm not taking any chances . . . Get a mirror.

MEREDITH (*Reaching into a purse*): I've got one here.

GOTTLIEB: Shine it in his face. He can't stand that.

(SHE *hesitates, then does*)

ATTENDANT (*Cringing, trying to hide*): Take that away. I don't want to see myself. A homely guy, with pock-marks.

TANDY (*Releasing* GOTTLIEB, *deflecting* MEREDITH's *mirror*): All right, wait a minute, I can't go through with this . . . Leave him alone . . .

ATTENDANT (*Gets himself together—then, as though feelings are really hurt*): Et tu, Gottlieb . . . (*Makes a move to* MEREDITH, *indicating it is her turn*)

MEREDITH: Au revoir, Mr. Tandy. Did I do all right with the mirror?

TANDY: You did fine, kid.

(MEREDITH *goes through the door*)

ATTENDANT (*To* TANDY): You couldn't stand that, right, to see God get wiped out . . . It gave you a funny feeling.

TANDY: I don't like to see anybody get wiped out . . . I'm notorious for breaking up fights . . . I once threw a guy through the window of a furniture store because somebody was picking on him and I didn't want him to get hurt.

ATTENDANT: You got a lot of nice qualities . . . Too bad I'm filled up. I'd let you work around here for a while . . . Listen, what are you giving yourself such a hard time for . . . Suppose, for a second, I let you out of here . . . What would you do? . . .

TANDY: What would I do? . . . Are you kidding? . . . What is this, a put-on? . . . You didn't hear me go on about my new life? My new style? The exciting world that's out there waiting for me? . . . This terrific new quiet girl friend who practically brings me the newspaper in her teeth—who watches me like a hawk for the slightest sign of sexual tension—and then *whop*—she's in there like a shot to drain it off and make me feel comfortable again . . . And if I feel like going out at four in the morning to get some eggs—she's right there at my side—because she comes from a tradition where the man is like a gypsy king and the woman is someone who drags mutton to him on her back, all the way up a hill. And all she ever hopes for is that he'll throw her a lousy mutton bone while she's sleeping in the dirt at his feet . . . And this is an intelligent girl, too . . . a Bryn Mawr girl . . . When I'm alone with her . . .

ATTENDANT: You like this girl . . .

TANDY: Like her? . . . Oh, I see what you mean . . . Yeah . . . if I'm so crazy about her, how come I'm constantly chasing chicks all over the place . . . All right, I'll admit to you that she's a little on the quiet side—that sometimes all that quiet drives me nuts . . . All right, let's face it, she's basically a dull girl. Terrific kid, loyal, faithful, brings you mutton, but the sparks don't fly . . . And it did cross my mind that maybe I'll find another girl who's got a little more pizazz . . . I'll give you that . . .

ATTENDANT: Another girl . . .

TANDY: Yeah. Another girl. Oh, I got ya', I got ya'—a new one isn't going to be the answer either . . . As delicious as she looks now, in two months I'm a little restless again . . . And that's the way it's got to be if I live to be a hundred . . . (*Trails off*) Look, I got to travel . . . I got to move around. And I'm all set to get rolling. There was a woman who used to take care of me when

I was little and she was born in Mukden, during the
. . . Chinese war . . . Very interesting woman, had a
lot to do with my future development. Well, she used
to describe a beautiful church to me where she went to
school, right in the middle of Mukden. I always
promised myself I'd get over there and see that church,
maybe carve my initials in one of the pews . . . And
that somehow that would round off the corners on Mrs.
Grainger's life . . . she's got a spinal condition . . . I
still write to her. Well, I can do that now. I can go
right over to Mukden and stand in the middle of that
church . . .

ATTENDANT: She wants you to go to Mukden . . .

TANDY: . . . Oh, I see what you're driving at—I don't have
to go to Mukden. I don't have to go 26,000 miles and
break my balls to show her I love her. I can stay right
here and carry out some of the proverbs she taught me
and it's just as good . . . You got a point there . . . All
right, forget Mukden . . . No more Mukden . . .

I got friends, terrific friends. We hang around this
bar called The Quonset Hut, run by a dyke, a rich
retired dyke. We hang around there, sometimes till five
in the morning, talking about Milton and the Brontë
sisters. These friends of mine are terrific people—
they're a little screwed up in their personal lives—most
of them have been divorced three or four times—but
very often those are the best people, the ones who get
divorced over and over . . . Anyway, I want to do a

lot more of that, hanging around this dyke bar till five in the morning with my divorced friends, talking about Milton and the Brontë sisters . . .

And I have to get back to my book. Now I know what you're going to say and I'm way ahead of you— that I have no real visceral interest in Charlemagne— that I just picked that subject because it has a prestige sound to it. Well, you're wrong. To me it's just a loosening-up process, a way of warming up the writing muscles so I can be ready for the real book I want to write on—Vasco da Gama and the Straits of Magellan. (*Weak little laugh as though aware* HE's *told a joke. No response from* ATTENDANT) No, seriously . . . you have to get the muscles limber . . . What you're saying is if I really wanted to write I'd stop crapping around with Charlemagne . . . I see what you mean . . . You get more prestige from a truly observed book about . . . cheeseburgers than you can from a schlock Charlemagne book . . . Boy, you really nailed that one down . . .

I'll tell you what, let me smoke a cigar, all right?

(*Takes one out;* ATTENDANT *has sat down and begun to arrange the cards for a game of solitaire*)

I get these from Switzerland from a guy who brings them in from Cuba. It costs you a little extra, but it's really worth it. They say you're supposed to stop smoking these when you get about half way down, but

I don't know. Sometimes I think the last half of the cigar is the best part.

I can tell a Havana cigar in one puff. It's not the tobacco so much as the rolling process they use. They have a secret rolling process that nobody's ever been able to pry away from the Cubans . . .

If it kills me I got to get back and have some more weekends with my daughter. Those weekends are the most beautiful part of my life now. I mean there's no more hassle . . . no more crazy marriage in the background . . . It all gets telescoped down to just me and her, hanging around together.

(*Looks at* ATTENDANT *for response, doesn't get one*)

. . . So you're asking me how come I'm always going crazy thinking up places to take her . . . How come I'm always dragging her to puppet shows . . . Well, all I can say is that it's the city's fault . . . Where the hell are you supposed to take a kid in the city . . . If we were out on a farm, it'd be a different story . . .

But I do see what you mean—Jesus, you really know how to zing it in there . . . what you're driving at is that I have to keep taking her places because I actually have nothing to say to her . . . Maybe I don't even like kids . . . She'd be better off staying home and hanging around with a pack of little girls . . . (*Handling cigar*) A guy once told me the reason for the special flavor of these Havana cigars is that the tobacco is

supposed to be rolled on the thighs of Cuban women . . .
Jesus, wouldn't that be something . . .

   I got to get out of here . . . I got to get out of here . . .
I got things to do . . .

     (ATTENDANT *continues his game of solitaire*
     —the last sound heard is the flicking of the
     cards . . .)
         CURTAIN

A NOTE ON THE TYPE

The text of this book was set on the Linotype in a face
called Times Roman, designed by Stanley Morison for
The Times (London) and first introduced by that newspaper in 1932.

Among typographers and designers of the twentieth
century, Stanley Morison has been a strong forming influ-
ence, as typographical adviser to the English Monotype
Corporation, as a director of two distinguished English
publishing houses, and as a writer of sensibility, erudition,
and keen practical sense.

*Composed, printed and bound by The Book Press,
Brattleboro, Vt.*

Typography and binding design by Virginia Tan.